BEFORE YOU MEET PRINCE CHARMING

STUDY GUIDE

BY REBEKAH MAY
& SARAH MALLY

Before You Meet Prince Charming Study Guide
Copyright © 2012 Tomorrow's Forefathers, Inc.

Published by
Tomorrow's Forefathers, Inc.
PO Box 11451
Cedar Rapids, Iowa 52410-1451
319-377-6728

Layout: Nickie Biegler

All Scripture references are from the King James Version.

Library of Congress Control Number: 2012932584
ISBN-10: 0-9719405-7-6
ISBN-13: 978-0-9719405-7-4

TABLE OF CONTENTS

NOTE TO READERS 5

CHAPTER ONE
Desire the Very Best Marriage 7

CHAPTER TWO
Dangers With the Dating System 11

CHAPTER THREE
Guard Your Heart 17

CHAPTER FOUR
Could He Be the One? 23

CHAPTER FIVE
Romantic Dreams 29

CHAPTER SIX
When God Says Wait 35

CHAPTER SEVEN
How Parents Can Help 39

CHAPTER EIGHT
Have a Life Purpose Bigger Than Marriage 43

CHAPTER NINE
Dreams Must Die 49

CHAPTER TEN
Reserved for One 55

CHAPTER ELEVEN
Delighting in the Lord 59

CHAPTER TWELVE
Know That God Arranges Marriages 63

INTERNET USAGE & MODERN TECHNOLOGY 69

NOTE TO READERS

If you're like most girls today, you have questions about guy/girl relationships. Lots of questions. This is a good thing! We should be willing to ask the difficult questions and seek out the biblical answers. We can't afford to simply follow the worldly patterns of our culture and hope that everything will turn out all right. We have been called to something better, something wondrous—the high calling of God in Christ Jesus (Philippians 3:14).

God's Word is filled with wisdom and counsel that is readily available for those who are seeking it. We were designed by God to have relationships (with Him and others), and only by studying His Word will we have a correct worldview of how each of these relationships should properly function to bring Him glory.

This study guide is not divided into daily assignments. I'd suggest covering one chapter per week. Please do not rush through the questions and Scripture readings! Take the time to dig deeper into Scripture and allow the Lord to captivate your heart and transform your thinking. His Word is our authority and our guide. If we want answers, we must be prepared to dig. The more time you invest in seeking Him, the more amazing things you'll discover about Him!

I'd encourage you to grab a friend, a group of friends, or your parents, and go through this study together. Accountability and fellowship are so important for spiritual growth. No matter who you're doing it with, I'd encourage you to share what you're learning with your parents and keep them informed about the commitments you are making.

Take the next several weeks to immerse yourself in God's Word, seeking to understand His heart and His ways. And in the process of searching the Scriptures and seeking answers, my prayer is that you'll find more than just answers to your questions—I pray that you'll find Him.

CHAPTER ONE

1. *W*hy did you decide to read this book? What are you hoping to learn from it?

2. *I*n the story, the grandmother commented that the princess was a princess in conduct as well as in lineage. What do you think she meant?

3. *D*uring the conversation between the princess and the alligator, what advice did the alligator give to the princess? Was it wise advice?

4. *A*s young women who are seeking to follow the Lord and His plan for our lives, we need Godly advice and counsel. Who has the Lord given you to provide guidance and protection in your life?

5. *A*re you currently submitting to their authority? If so, how?

6. *Are* you personally committed to embracing specific safeguards of protection? Or are you only tolerating them?

7. *Why* is it important to desire the very best marriage?

8. *On* page 22, Sarah states, "The decisions we make in our youth play a huge role in determining our future." How have you observed this to be true in your life and in the lives of those you know?

9. *Read* Psalm 119:9-11. How can we keep our way pure?

10. *Describe* the two kinds of purity mentioned in this chapter and the differences between them. Why is it important that we understand this as we are beginning this study?

11. According to Isaiah 1:18, does the Lord offer to us innocent or cleansed purity? This verse clearly states that it is the power of Jesus' blood that washes away our sins. In light of that truth, can our sins ever be too great for Christ to cleanse and make pure?

12. Read 1 John 3:1-2. Knowing that we are made pure by the blood of Christ is a comforting and exciting truth. We have been chosen to be daughters of the King of kings! Now read 1 John 3:3. Having that knowledge, how should we respond?

13. According to 2 Chronicles 16:9, whom is the Lord searching for? What special promise does He make to them?

14. On page 26, there is a description of the phrase "Radiant Purity." How would you explain this in your own words?

15. Why will a radiantly pure young woman stand out in the world today?

16. *Three* presuppositions are listed on page 26. What are they? Do you agree with them?

SUGGESTED ASSIGNMENT: READ THE BOOK OF 1 JOHN.

MEMORIZE REVELATION 19:7.

Let us be glad and rejoice, and give honour to Him: for the marriage of the Lamb is come, and His wife hath made herself ready.

Chapter Two

1. At the beginning of this chapter, the princess expressed her desire to go to the Spring Fair and mingle with the young men and women. What reasons did she give for wanting to go?

2. Have you ever struggled with similar desires? How should we respond if we feel that our parents are being overly cautious?

3. The princess was struggling with the desire to fit in with her friends. Read Proverbs 29:25. What does our Heavenly Father say about seeking the approval of our friends? According to this verse, what is the opposite of seeking their approval?

4. On what should we base our worldview and approach to guy/girl relationships? Who is the ultimate Authority? See 2 Timothy 3:16-17.

5. On page 37, we see the contrasts between the world's way of thinking in regard to relationships and God's plan and desire for our relationships. Read Galatians 5:16-17. Which way do you think our flesh naturally gravitates? Why?

6. Now read Galatians 5:18-26. What are some of the evidences of a life controlled by the flesh? What character qualities will be displayed by a life controlled by the Spirit?

FLESH	SPIRIT

7. In your own words, what does it mean to walk in the Spirit? How can you put that into practice today?

8. In this chapter, we have identified many dangers of the typical American dating system. From your own perspective, what consequences of dating have you experienced in your life or observed in the lives of those around you?

9. Read 1 Peter 1:14-16 and 2 Corinthians 6:16-18. No matter what our culture deems normal or acceptable, we have a higher calling. According to these verses, what have we been called to and why?

10. Read 1 Timothy 4:12 and 2 Timothy 2:22. What special charge and command does the Lord give to young people?

11. Many girls make the excuse that they will never be able to get to know someone if they do not date him. According to Scripture, is this a valid argument? What are the benefits of observing the character of a young man in a group environment such as when he is with his family, involved in church activities, and serving in ministry projects?

12. After considering these things, what personal commitments to Christ are you ready to make in regard to your relationships? What specific boundaries and safeguards are you seeking to put into practice? Write them down and discuss them with your parents.

MEMORIZE GALATIANS 5:16.

This I say then, Walk in the Spirit, and ye shall not fulfil the lust of the flesh.

Wherewithal shall a young man cleanse his way? by taking heed thereto according to thy word. With my whole heart have I sought thee: O let me not wander from thy commandments. Thy word have I hid in mine heart, that I might not sin against thee. Psalm 119:9-11

COMPLETE THE ASSIGNMENT ON PAGE 41 OF *BEFORE YOU MEET PRINCE CHARMING*

○ ○ ○ ○ ○ ○ ○ ○ ○ ○ ○ ○ ○ ○ ○ ○ ○ ○ ○ ○

CHAPTER THREE

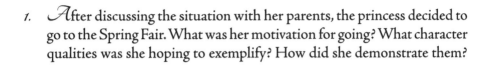

1.   After discussing the situation with her parents, the princess decided to go to the Spring Fair. What was her motivation for going? What character qualities was she hoping to exemplify? How did she demonstrate them?

2.   Sir Eloquence was very kind and friendly to the princess. Do you think that the princess handled the situation correctly? Why or why not?

3.   Chapter three explains six ways that we, as young ladies, can guard our hearts. Which one do you think will be the hardest to put into practice in your life? Why?

4.   Consider your current friendships with young men; are they casual? Are there any changes you need to make in the ways you interact with young men?

5.   Read Romans 13:14. How can we avoid making provision for our flesh? How should we respond to situations that may cause us to form emotional bonds?

6. Read Philippians 2:1-11. As we seek to be followers of Christ, what should our attitude be? How does this relate to our relationships with others?

7. Read 1 Thessalonians 4:1-9. According to Strong's Concordance, the word "defraud" in verse six can also be translated "to be covetous, over reaching, desiring more, to get an advantage or eager to gain." Take a minute to think about your recent attitudes, words, and actions around young men. Are you treating your brothers in Christ with respect and pointing them to Jesus? Have you been defrauding them without realizing it?

8. Read Ephesians 6:1-2. What does it mean to honor your parents? What will we miss out on if we don't seek their advice?

9. Is there anything that you have been hiding from your parents and need to confess? Read Proverbs 28:13. What is the consequence of hiding sin? What is the blessing of confessing and repenting of sin?

10. According to Proverbs 18:21, what kind of power is contained in our words? What are some topics to avoid when talking with friends? What are wholesome and encouraging topics to discuss?

11. As princesses of the King, we must rid our lives of polluting influences. Prayerfully consider your choice of movies, television, music, Internet usage, books and magazines.
    - *Are these things encouraging you in your walk with Christ, or are they causing you to become distracted?*
    - *Are they sources of temptation to sin?*
    - *Are they causing you to stumble?*
    - *Is there anything that you need to remove from your life? If so, discuss it with your parents and commit to removing the polluting influences immediately.*

MEMORIZE PROVERBS 4:23.

Keep thy heart with all diligence; for out of it are the issues of life.

COMPLETE THE ASSIGNMENT ON PAGES 63-64 OF *BEFORE YOU MEET PRINCE CHARMING*. HERE ARE SOME VERSES TO HELP YOU GET STARTED:

1 Kings 3:9, 12 _____

_____

_____

2 Chronicles 16:9 _____

_____

_____

2 Chronicles 34:27 _____

_____

_____

Psalm 7:10 _____

_____

_____

Psalm 34:18 _____

_____

_____

Psalm 51:10 _____

_____

_____

Psalm 119:80 _____

_____

_____

Proverbs 17:22 _____

_____

_____

Matthew 5:8_____

_____

_____

Matthew 11:29_____

_____

_____

Ephesians 4:32 _____

_____

_____

2 Timothy 2:22_____

_____

_____

James 4:8_____

_____

_____

1 Peter 1:22 _____

_____

_____

_____

_____

_____

_____

_____

_____

_____

_____

CHAPTER FOUR

1. *S*ir Eloquence was not deemed a suitable match for the princess. What character flaws did the king and the princess notice in Sir Eloquence?

2. *T*hough it may seem harmless, flattery is a very serious sin. Read Psalm 12:3 and Proverbs 26:28. What does the Lord say about flattery? What are some consequences that would result from beginning a relationship with a young man who has flattering lips? How does a person's motive behind their words indicate whether the words are flattery or genuine encouragement?

3. *R*ead 2 Corinthians 6:14. According to this verse, is it ever okay to consider developing a close relationship with (and/or marrying) a non-Christian young man?

4. *R*ead 1 Corinthians 7:34, 39 and Ephesians 5:22-24. Why is it important to marry not just a Christian, but a strong Christian? What are the benefits and blessings of doing so?

5. *R*ead 1 Samuel 16:6-7. According to these verses, what is important to the Lord? Why is it unwise to look only at the outward appearance (the physical appearance, actions, words, etc.) of a young man?

6. *A*re you committed to working with your parents to discern the genuine character and vision of any potential suitor? If not, what is keeping you from making that commitment?

7. *R*ead Matthew 7:16-20, John 13:35, and 15:8. According to these verses, how do we demonstrate that we are disciples of Christ? How do we discern between those **who are** and those **who are not** true disciples of Christ?

8. *W*hy do you think so many girls settle for less than God's best in whom they marry?

9. *A*re you willing to wait until spiritual maturity and genuine fruit are evident in a young man's life?

10. *H*ave you ever wondered if your standards are too high? Read Psalm 19:7-9 and Isaiah 55:8-9. Where should our standards come from?

11. *R*ead Proverbs 31:10-31, 1 Timothy 2:9-15, 3:11, 5:14 and Titus 2:4-5. What are the characteristics of a godly wife? (examples: trustworthy, diligent, industrious, etc.)

12. *G*o through the list of "self-evaluation" questions on pages 80-81 of *Before You Meet Prince Charming*.
   + Are there areas that you have not fully surrendered to the Lord?

   + What specific areas need improvement? Write those specific areas below and ask the Lord to give you wisdom in how to change and grow in His grace.

MEMORIZE 2 CORINTHIANS 6:14.

Be ye not unequally yoked together
with unbelievers: for what
fellowship hath righteousness
with unrighteousness? and what
communion hath light
with darkness?

Thy word have I hid in mine heart, that I might not sin against thee. Psalm 119:9-11 Wherewithal shall a young man cleanse his way? by taking heed thereto according to thy word. With my whole heart have I sought thee: O let me not wander from thy commandments. Thy word have I hid in mine heart

COMPLETE THE ASSIGNMENT ON PAGE 83 OF *BEFORE YOU MEET PRINCE CHARMING.*

List some qualifications you are looking for in a husband.

ESSENTIAL	DESIRABLE
(qualities that are requirements)	(important, but not necessarily a requirement)

ESSENTIAL	DESIRABLE
•	•
•	•
•	•
•	•
•	•
•	•
•	•
•	•
•	•
•	•
•	•

(feel free to continue on a separate sheet)

What character traits do you admire in great men in Scripture that you also desire in a future husband?

Name	Verse	Qualities
Job	Job 1:1	
Caleb	Joshua 14:14	
David	1 Samuel 16:18	
Daniel	Daniel 1:8	
Stephen	Acts 6	
_____	_____	
_____	_____	

CHAPTER FIVE

1. *T*hough the princess was firm in her commitment to not attend any of the balls or worldly gatherings of the young people in the village, she was afraid her friends did not understand. What advice did the queen give to the princess?

2. *R*ead 1 Peter 2:21-23. According to these verses, what should our response be when others reject us? What example has Christ left us to follow?

3. *A*fter seeing the shallowness of character that Sir Eloquence possessed, the princess noticed many admirable qualities in Sir Valiant and allowed her thoughts to wander. Read 2 Corinthians 10:5. What are some practical ways you can bring every thought captive to the obedience of Christ?

4. *O*ur thoughts are not "neutral." It does matter what we spend our time thinking about. Read Philippians 4:8. What kind of thoughts should we have? List a few examples.

5. *R*ead Psalm 19:14. Write this verse in your own words as a prayer to the Lord.

6. *R*ead Joshua 1:8 and Psalm 1:1-3. What promises does the Lord make to those who will meditate on His Word?

7. *P*age 93 explains four things that we should **not** do when we've noticed a young man and are attracted to him. What are they? Which of those areas do you think will be the most difficult to avoid?

8. *W*e must guard against having a "dating spirit," which will hinder our whole-hearted devotion to Christ. It's not simply our actions that matter—it's the attitudes behind those actions. It's not the "terms" we use that make the difference (i.e. courtship vs. dating), it's the motives of our heart. Examples of having a dating spirit:
   - *allowing your thoughts and affections to be focused on romantic dreams*
   - *cultivating emotional attachments*
   - *trying to get a young man to "notice" you*

• *wishing you could have a boyfriend and getting as close to it as possible without actually "dating"*
• *giving away pieces of your heart by sharing emotions prematurely*
• *spending lots of time together without actually dating*
• *seeking to attract attention to ourselves in our dress, attitudes and words*

Prayerfully examine your heart. Have you allowed a "spirit of dating" to creep in? If so, in what ways?

9. According to Psalm 73:25-26 and Song of Solomon 8:4, what commitments should we make that will help us to guard against a "spirit of dating"?

10. Explain the "springboard method" of dealing with wrong thoughts. Who or what will be your prayer target? On which Scripture verses will you meditate?

11. Have you ever spoken with your parents about a crush before? If you have, what helped you to do so? If not, what hindered you from doing so? List some of the benefits of sharing our hearts and feelings with our parents. Do you have something that you need to share with them now? When are you going to tell them? What are you going to say?

Memorize Philippians 4:8.

Finally, brethren, whatsoever things are true, whatsoever things are honest, whatsoever things are just, whatsoever things are pure, whatsoever things are lovely, whatsoever things are of good report; if there be any virtue, and if there be any praise, think on these things.

COMPLETE THE ASSIGNMENT ON PAGE 99 OF *BEFORE YOU MEET PRINCE CHARMING*.

LIE:_____

TRUTH:_____

_____

LIE:_____

TRUTH:_____

_____

LIE:_____

TRUTH:_____

_____

LIE:_____

TRUTH:_____

_____

LIE:_____

TRUTH:_____

_____

LIE:_____

TRUTH:_____

_____

LIE:_____

TRUTH:_____

_____

LIE:_____

TRUTH:_____

_____

CHAPTER SIX

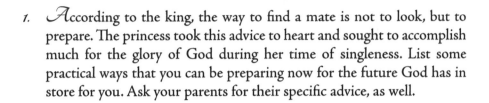

1. *A*ccording to the king, the way to find a mate is not to look, but to prepare. The princess took this advice to heart and sought to accomplish much for the glory of God during her time of singleness. List some practical ways that you can be preparing now for the future God has in store for you. Ask your parents for their specific advice, as well.

2. *H*owever, even in the midst of her preparations, the princess allowed a seed to begin to grow in her heart. What was that seed?

3. *L*ook up synonyms and antonyms of the word "content." In regard to marriage, which of these words best portrays the condition of your heart right now?

4. *R*ead Philippians 4:11-13, 1 Timothy 6:6, and Hebrews 13:5. How can you be demonstrating contentment in your life this week?

5. *L*ike the princess experienced, feelings of discontentment often lead to self-pity, loneliness, despair, hopelessness, and doubts about the Lord and the truth of Scripture. Have you ever experienced this cycle in your life? Read Psalm 84. What truths are contained in this chapter that will help you to develop contentment?

6. *R*eview the consequences of failing to wait patiently for the Lord (listed on page 111). Share a personal testimony of a time when you experienced one of these consequences and the lessons the Lord taught you through that circumstance.

7. *R*ead Lamentations 3:21-26. What do these verses reveal about the character of God? What does it mean to "quietly wait"?

8. The commands to "wait on the Lord" and "hope in Him" are often found together in Scripture. (See Psalm 130:5 and Romans 8:24-25.) What do you think is the significance of this?

9. Read Titus 2:11-14. As we wait for the "blessed hope," what instructions do we have from the Lord?

10. What is your biggest fear as you wait for the Lord to bring your future spouse? What Scripture verses combat that lie with the Truth?

11. The more we come to understand the love of God for us, the less we will need to be dependent on the love that we desire in a boyfriend or future husband. Read 1 John 4:15-19. How is fear cast out of our lives? According to these verses, how are we "made perfect in love"?

12. Read Psalm 27:14, 40:1-3, and 62:1-8. What blessings are promised to those who wait? What opportunities has God given you to serve Him while you are waiting?

COMPLETE THE ASSIGNMENT ON PAGES 120-121 OF *BEFORE YOU MEET PRINCE CHARMING.*

Who will you purpose to encourage? _____

What are some ways that you will reach out to her?

When will you do it?

MEMORIZE PSALM 84:11-12.

For the LORD God is a sun and shield: the LORD will give grace and glory: no good thing will He withhold from them that walk uprightly. O LORD of hosts, blessed is the man that trusteth in Thee.

CHAPTER SEVEN

1. *In* his conversation with the princess, the king quoted Proverbs 22:3. Read that verse again. What does it mean to be prudent?

2. *Read* Romans 13:1 and Ephesians 6:1-3. How are these verses encouraging and comforting to us as we seek to honor our imperfect parents? Are there past hurts in your relationship with your parents for which you need to forgive them?

3. *We* do not have perfect earthly parents, but we do have a perfect Heavenly Father! Read Hebrews 12:5-11. Though His discipline is not always pleasant, what are the benefits we reap from correctly responding to it?

4. *How* would you describe your relationship with your parents? Use 10-20 words.

5. *Are* you honoring them in your attitudes, actions, and words? List a few areas in which you need improvement in your relationship.

6. The book of Proverbs has a lot to say about honoring our parents. Read Proverbs chapters 3-4 and write down several benefits of heeding our parents' instructions and the consequences of spurning their advice.

BENEFITS	CONSEQUENCES

7. The enemy is seeking to pervert anything that he can and the area of clothing is no exception. Some of his strategies are:
   - *To expose—creating immodesty, temptation, and lust*
   - *To distort the roles of men and women—urging men to try to be like women, and women to be like men*
   - *To distract—directing our focus to unimportant, outward things rather than the inner qualities which truly matter*
   - *To ensnare—making people slaves of fashion trends and fads*
   - *To breed discontentment—causing people to believe they need to have the right outward appearance in order to be happy*

   Examine your life. Have you been ensnared by any of these strategies? How?

8. Read Proverbs 31:30, 1 Timothy 2:9-10 and 1 Peter 3:3-4. What does the Lord say about our outward appearance?

9. Read 1 Corinthians 6:19-20. Do we belong to ourselves? Do we have the right to dress in any way we want? Why, or why not?

10. One important way that we can honor both the Lord and our parents is by dressing modestly and femininely. Though the world wants us to follow the latest styles and trends of the fashion industry, we should not be looking to the world for our standard of purity! Consider your current wardrobe. Does your clothing reflect that your heart is pure before the Lord and that you are honoring your parents? Are you bringing glory to the Lord by what you wear?

11. Make a list of some of the benefits of dressing modestly. How does it affect the following people:
   + Ourselves?

   + Our parents?

   + Young men around us?

   + Young ladies around us?

   + Unbelievers we meet?

   + Our future husband?

12. Have you committed to send any young men who express interest in you to your father? Have you discussed this with your father? Pages 130-131 list seven reasons to do so; can you think of any others?

13. Read Ephesians 5:21-33 and 1 Peter 3:1-6. How will learning to honor your father now benefit your future marriage? What practical ways have you found to honor and build your relationship with your father?

14. One way that we can develop a heart of submission toward our parents is by being in prayer for them. Are you currently committed to consistently praying for your parents? Ask your parents for specific prayer requests and write them below.

COMPLETE THE ASSIGNMENT ON PAGE 140 OF *BEFORE YOU MEET PRINCE CHARMING* OR WRITE A LETTER OF GRATEFULNESS TO ONE OR BOTH OF YOUR PARENTS.

MEMORIZE PROVERBS 23:26.

My son, give me thine heart, and let thine eyes observe my ways.

Chapter Eight

1. *R*ead Matthew 6:33. In your own words, what do you think it means to "seek first the kingdom of God, and His righteousness"?

2. *W*hen others see your life, what evidence will they see that you are seeking the Lord above all else? Explain your answer.

3. *T*he king commissioned Sir Valiant, using the weapons of truth and righteousness, to fight against the dragon called Lies and the giant named Temptation. In the same way, we are called to fight against lies and temptations in our lives. According to Ephesians 6:10-17, what specific spiritual armor have we been given? Write down one example of a practical way to use your "armor."

4. *W*hat enemies do you think are most dangerous in our nation—the physical ones or the spiritual ones? Terrorists or Hollywood? What are some ways that we can fight the true battles in this land? Think with creativity and faith when writing your ideas.

5. *R*ead John 15:1-12. According to this passage, what brings us true joy and fulfillment?

6. *Th*e seed of Discontent was continuing to grow in the princess's heart. Examine your own heart. Have you allowed discontentment to grow in any area of your life? If so, how?

7. *H*ave you entertained thoughts of self-pity? When was the last time you started feeling sorry for yourself? Read Isaiah 64:8, Jeremiah 18:1-6 and Romans 9:20. Why is it an attack against the character of God when we complain about our circumstances?

8. *R*ead Psalm 9:10 and Isaiah 49:15-16. How do these verses combat the fear of being forgotten by the Lord?

9. *R*ead Ephesians 5:15-17. How does the Lord want us to walk? How should we view the time He has given us?

10. The years of our youth and singleness can never be lived again once they are over. Read Psalm 90:12. Do you have a vision for what the Lord could do through your life? What is something you could do to further His kingdom:

   + Today?

   + This month?

   + This year?

11. We each have different struggles in redeeming our time. What are some areas in your life where you find yourself consistently wasting time? On the Internet (Facebook, Twitter, email, blogs)? Watching television? Reading romance novels? Texting? Other?

12. Knowing your weakness in those areas, what specific steps will you take to build safeguards for yourself? Who are you going to ask to keep you accountable?

13. What is your life purpose? Support your answer with Scripture.

14. *If* it was the Lord's will for you to serve Him as a single woman your whole life, how would you feel about that? What helps you deal with fears about the possibility of never getting married?

15. *Pages* 162-163 list five main points to remember from this chapter. What are they?

*M*EMORIZE MATTHEW 6:33.

But seek ye first the kingdom of God, and His righteousness; and all these things shall be added unto you.

COMPLETE THE ASSIGNMENT ON PAGES 163-164 OF *BEFORE YOU MEET PRINCE CHARMING.*

+ $\mathcal{P}$ray and ask the Lord what messages He has entrusted to you which He wants you to share with others.

+ $\mathcal{T}$he gospel is the primary message for each of us to share. What is a creative way you can share the gospel using your testimony or illustrations from your own life?

+ $\mathcal{W}$hat other needs specifically burden you?

+ $\mathcal{W}$hat major lessons has the Lord taught you which you could share with others?

+ $\mathcal{W}$hat verses has God used in your life which you could be sharing with others?

$\mathcal{C}$hoose at least one of these messages to share with at least one person this week!

CHAPTER NINE

1. After renewing her commitment to wait on the Lord, the princess found herself wrestling with her thoughts once again. Can you relate to her situation? Write one area that you seem to struggle in most often. Pray and ask the Lord for His specific wisdom and strength to overcome!

2. The queen gave her daughter a wise answer by explaining that struggles are a necessary part of life. Read 2 Corinthians 4:17-18 and 12:9-10 and 1 Peter 4:12-16 and 5:6-11. What should our attitude be toward our trials? List a few benefits of going through struggles.

3. Read Hebrews 2:17-18 and 4:14-16. What character qualities of Christ do you see in these verses? How do these verses encourage us during trials?

4. According to Philippians 3:7-10, what should be our one desire?

5. Read Romans 12:1-2 and Hebrews 12:1-3. What action is required on our part? What does the phrase "living sacrifice" imply? What must we do before we can run with perseverance?

6. In the hymn, *Trust and Obey*, the fourth verse reads, "But we never can prove the delights of His love until all on the altar we lay." In your own words, what does that sentence mean?

7. Have you purposed in your heart to wait for the Lord to arrange all the details of your future marriage?

8. Write down some of your specific expectations and dreams. (For example, do you expect to be married at a certain age? Meet your future spouse a certain way? Have a certain number of children? Etc.) Prayerfully surrender those desires to the Lord, knowing that His plans are best!

9. It takes faith to let go of our dreams and trust the Lord's timing and ways. According to Hebrews 11:1 and 6, what is faith?

10. Often, we cling tightly to our dreams and plans because we do not trust the Lord and believe His word. Read Matthew 13:58 and Hebrews 3:12-19. What resulted from unbelief?

11. Now read Genesis 18:14, 21:1-2 and Romans 4:16-22. What resulted from belief?

12. Does God ever delay? Is His timing ever late? Read Hebrews 10:35-39. What is our responsibility as we wait on Him?

13. In Matthew 26:39, Jesus displayed the ultimate example of complete surrender to the will of the Father. Do we have any "right" to hold on to our own dreams and desires? As we follow Christ's example, what should be the desire of our heart?

14. Read Luke 14:27 and 33. What is required to be a disciple of Christ?

15. Why do you think the Lord asks us to surrender everything to Him, even the good desires of our hearts?

MEMORIZE MATTHEW 16:25.

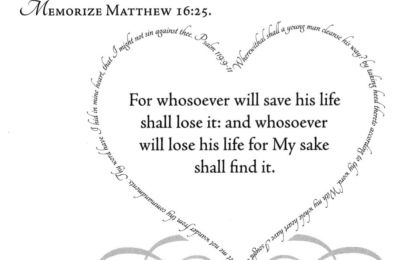

For whosoever will save his life shall lose it: and whosoever will lose his life for My sake shall find it.

COMPLETE THE ASSIGNMENT ON PAGE 178 OF *BEFORE YOU MEET PRINCE CHARMING*.

CHAPTER TEN

1. In her conversation with the alligator, the princess said, "It is not an earthly knight for whom I ultimately save myself but a heavenly One." Is this your desire, as well? What are the dangers of saving yourself only to gain an "earthly knight"?

2. What does it mean to be emotionally pure?

3. Why is emotional purity just as important as physical purity?

4. What aspect of emotional purity do you find yourself struggling with the most?

5. Read Psalm 62:5-8. When you are discouraged or struggling to control your emotions, what should you do?

6. Pouring yourself out in service to others is a great antidote to discouragement. According to Proverbs 11:25 and Isaiah 58:10-11, who will be satisfied?

7. What thoughts and actions would characterize a young lady who is "merely trying to avoid the worst"? What thoughts and actions would characterize a young lady who is "desiring to achieve the very best"?

8. List some "firsts" that you are committed to saving.

9. Read 1 Corinthians 6:12-20 and 7:4. What do these verses say regarding physical purity?

10. What should be our primary motivation for purity (see page 193)?

11. What are some of the earthly rewards and some of the spiritual rewards for choosing the way of purity?

12. Read John 4:9-30, 39 and 8:1-11. Is it ever too late to begin walking in purity before the Lord? How did the Lord use the testimony of these women for His glory?

13. Read Psalm 51. What should our response be when we sin? What does the Lord promise to do?

14. Read Luke 15:11-24. In this parable, what do we learn about our Heavenly Father?

15. According to Psalm 34:18 and Isaiah 57:15, what kind of heart is the Lord looking for?

16. Why is it not okay for us to just try and forget past mistakes and move on?

17. Read Proverbs 28:13. Why is it necessary to confess and "uproot" our sin and not take it lightly? Read 1 John 1:7 and 9. What does God promise when we choose to do so?

18. We have all sinned and made mistakes. Satan would like nothing better than for us to believe that it is too late, that we have messed up too much to ever be forgiven and restored by Christ. We must not allow ourselves to believe these lies! Read Isaiah 55:7, Romans 5:1-11, 2 Corinthians 5:17-21, and Hebrews 9:11-15. What has Christ done for us?

COMPLETE THE ASSIGNMENT ON PAGE 198 OF *BEFORE YOU MEET PRINCE CHARMING*.

QUESTION:_____

ANSWER:_____

QUESTION:_____

ANSWER:_____

QUESTION:_____

ANSWER:_____

QUESTION:_____

ANSWER:_____

QUESTION:_____

ANSWER:_____

MEMORIZE 1 THESSALONIANS 4:3-4.

For this is the will of God, even your sanctification, that ye should abstain from fornication: That every one of you should know how to possess his vessel in sanctification and honour;

Thy word have I hid in mine heart, that I might not sin against thee. Psalm 119:9-11 Wherewithal shall a young man cleanse his way? By taking heed thereto according to thy word. With my whole heart have I sought thee: O let me not wander from thy commandments.

CHAPTER ELEVEN

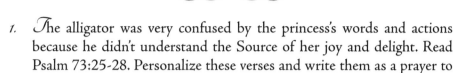

1. *The* alligator was very confused by the princess's words and actions because he didn't understand the Source of her joy and delight. Read Psalm 73:25-28. Personalize these verses and write them as a prayer to the Lord.

2. *The* One who created our desires is the only One who can ultimately fulfill them. Are you feeling restless and longing for love? Read Psalm 17:15, 36:7-9, and Proverbs 19:23. What does it mean to have your heart established in the love of Christ?

3. *Many* people have an equation in their heart. They think, "Christ plus _____ will make me truly happy." Are you allowing such an equation in your life? What are you looking to besides Christ to bring true fulfillment?

4. *Why* is it so important that we find our satisfaction in Christ? What are some consequences of looking to people to fulfill our desires, instead of to the Lord?

5. Read Isaiah 43:10-11 and Jeremiah 9:23-24. What relationship should be our priority? What does the Lord desire for our relationship with Him?

6. Read Psalm 63:1-8. How did the Psalmist demonstrate his hunger and thirst for the Lord? How are you demonstrating your hunger and thirst for Christ?

7. In Revelation 2:4-5, what rebuke did Jesus give to the church of Ephesus? Could this rebuke be addressed to you today? What should be your response if you have "left your first love"?

8. Jesus is given many different names and titles throughout Scripture. The princess mentions several of them in her conversation with the alligator. Look up these passages of Scripture and write down the specific names/titles given to Jesus:

   • John 8:12

   • John 15:1

   • Isaiah 9:6

   • Revelation 22:16

* Psalm 23:1

* Psalm 28:7

* Psalm 71:3

* Isaiah 54:5

* Isaiah 62:5

There are many more you can search for on your own!

9. Look through the list of spiritual parallels on pages 208-209. Marriage is an earthly relationship with spiritual significance. What is the earthly marriage relationship designed by God to reflect? How does this truth impact the way you view marriage?

10. List some things you look forward to receiving from your husband someday (love, companionship, gifts, security, etc.) and then think about how the Lord can and does fulfill those desires.

11. When has the Lord reminded you of His love in a special way? Explain.

12. This chapter lists eleven ways that we can fall in love with Jesus. Prayerfully look through this list. Which area will you especially focus on developing in your life right now?

COMPLETE THE ASSIGNMENT ON PAGE 216 OF *BEFORE YOU MEET PRINCE CHARMING.*

MEMORIZE PSALM 37:4.

Delight thyself also in the LORD: and He shall give thee the desires of thine heart.

CHAPTER TWELVE

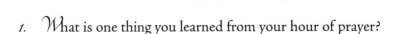

1. *W*hat is one thing you learned from your hour of prayer?

2. *N*o two courtship stories will be alike; God has a unique plan for you! According to Psalm 40:5 and 139:17, do we need to worry that the Lord might forget about us? Describe His thoughts toward us.

3. *I*t is unwise to compare ourselves to others and wish that our life (and our love story) was similar to theirs. We must not allow any jealousy or bitterness in our hearts! Read Hebrews 12:15 and James 3:13-18. What consequences result from harboring bitterness? What character qualities are displayed by a wise woman?

4. *R*ead Romans 8:28 and 1 Corinthians 2:9. Though we may have times of uncertainty and pain on this adventurous path of purity, what encouragement do these verses hold?

5. What is the proper sequence when two people join together in marriage (see page 228)? What order does the world typically follow?

6. The spiritual and the physical are rivals. Keeping that in mind, read Romans 6:11-14. Because we are in Christ, how should we live? What should we yield to the Lord?

7. Pages 229-232 mention six general guidelines for coming together with a life partner. What are they? Why is it beneficial for our relationships to follow this general order?

8. What next step should we take as we wait for our Prince Charming (see page 233)?

9. "The way to find a mate is not to look, but to prepare!" This concept cannot be emphasized enough. Do you have a "seeking" mindset or a "preparing" mindset? How is that seen in your life?

10. Are you currently involved in ministry? If so, what ministries and how are you involved? Do you feel the Lord is calling you to any other type of ministry, as well?

11. When was the last time you shared the gospel with someone? Do you feel like you need more training in evangelism? (If so, we suggest you read *Will Our Generation Speak?* by Grace Mally.)

12. Read Matthew 28:18-20. Who are you currently discipling and encouraging in the Lord?

13. Read 1 Corinthians 7:32-35. What ministry can you have to your family right now? How can you be a servant to them?

14. What unique ministry opportunities are available for single women?

15. According to James 1:22-25, what should our response be upon hearing the truth of God's Word?

16. Write out a prayer of thanksgiving to the Lord for all that He has promised to do as you wait for His perfect timing.

MEMORIZE EPHESIANS 3:20-21.

Now unto Him that is able to do exceeding abundantly above all that we ask or think, according to the power that worketh in us, unto Him be glory in the church by Christ Jesus throughout all ages, world without end. Amen.

COMPLETE THE ASSIGNMENT ON PAGE 238 OF *BEFORE YOU MEET PRINCE CHARMING*.

Here are some questions that would be good to ask:

+ In what ways do you wish you had been better prepared for marriage and motherhood?

+ What is one specific trait of godliness (patience, joyfulness, kindness, orderliness, etc.) in which you think it would be important for me to improve before I get married?

+ What is one specific household skill that you suggest I learn and develop during this season of my life?

+ What is one of the most important lessons that you have learned from being a mom?

INTERNET USAGE & MODERN TECHNOLOGY

1. *W*ould you say that your use of media and modern technology has had a positive impact on your relationship with the Lord or had the opposite effect?

2. *H*ave you embraced specific safeguards? If so, what are they? Review the list of possible safeguards on pages 258-260. Are there any additional safeguards you would like to put into practice?

3. *H*ave you ever been secretive on the Internet or cell phone and kept things from your parents? Are you currently hiding things that you don't want them to see? Review Proverbs 28:13. When will you confess those things to them?

4. *D*o you think that the Lord is pleased by your use of media (cell phone, texting, blogs, news outlets, Facebook, Twitter, television, magazines, etc.)?

5. *H*ave you ever found yourself lowering your standards on the Internet or cell phone because "everyone else is doing it"?

6. Read Proverbs 11:13, Matthew 12:36-37, Hebrews 4:13, and James 3:1-12. Explain several reasons why we must pay close attention to our words (whether spoken or written).

7. How much time did you spend online this week? What are some things that you have wanted to do but couldn't, because you were "too busy"?

8. Read the following verses about time: 2 Corinthians 5:6-10, Galatians 6:7-10, and James 4:14-17. What would be some practical ways to apply the principles found in these verses in regard to Internet usage?

9. Ephesians 5:15-16 tells us to redeem the time because the days are evil. The word "redeem" means to "buy back." What does it mean to redeem time? List some ways we can do this.

10. Make a list of several ways that you could use social media to further the kingdom of God and encourage the Body of Christ.

11. Read 1 Corinthians 6:12. Are you in any way being mastered by modern technology? If so, how?

12. Considering all of these things, do you need to make any changes in your use of modern technology? If so, what?

$\mathcal{Q}$uestionnaire
INTERNET USAGE & MODERN TECHNOLOGY

Rate yourself 1-5 in each of the following areas.

1. *This is a major struggle for me.*
2. *I struggle with this quite a lot.*
3. *I struggle with this sometimes, but not that much.*
4. *I only struggle with this a little bit.*
5. *This is not really a struggle for me – in fact, this is probably one of my strengths.*

☐ Controlling the amount of time I spend on the computer or cell phone

☐ Wasting time on unimportant, useless things (like online games or quizzes, browsing YouTube videos, etc.)

☐ Seeking to gain attention for myself through frequent emails, Facebook status updates, Tweets, or texting

☐ Using the Internet to gossip or complain about others

☐ Being open and honest with my parents about Internet and cell phone content and usage

☐ Pointing others to Christ through what I write and say

☐ Desiring "friendship" with as many people as possible to fuel my self-esteem

☐ Putting my family's needs and schedule before my own time online

☐ Keeping my online interactions pure and appropriate

☐ Constantly checking my email account and becoming worried and upset if I can't

☐ Wishing I had the latest version of computers or cell phones

☐ Being hypocritical in my online interactions by writing to impress others and gain their good opinion

☐ Making it my priority to spend time in God's Word before time online

☐ Finding time for the most important priorities in life—reading & memorizing God's Word, investing in family & others, witnessing, etc.

☐ Justifying relationships with young men online, because it's not actually "dating"

☐ Honoring and obeying the counsel and instruction of my parents in my Internet and cell phone usage

☐ Guarding my eyes and avoiding inappropriate content at all cost